W9-CEG-298

Growing Readers

New Hanover County Public Library

Purchased with
New Hanover County Smart Start Funds

Character Education

Prudence

by Lucia Raatma

Consultant:
Madonna Murphy, Ph.D.
Associate Professor of Education
University of St. Francis, Joliet, Illinois
Author, *Character Education in America's
Blue Ribbon Schools*

Bridgestone Books
an imprint of Capstone Press
Mankato, Minnesota

NEW HANOVER COUNTY
PUBLIC LIBRARY
201 CHESTNUT STREET
WILMINGTON, N C 2840

Bridgestone Books are published by Capstone Press
151 Good Counsel Drive, P.O. Box 669, Mankato, Minnesota 56002
http://www.capstone-press.com

Copyright © 2000 Capstone Press. All rights reserved.
No part of this book may be reproduced without written permission from the publisher.
The publisher takes no responsibility for the use of any of the materials
or methods described in this book, nor for the products thereof.
Printed in the United States of America.

Library of Congress Cataloging-in-Publication Data
Raatma, Lucia.
    Prudence/by Lucia Raatma.
    p. cm—(Character education)
    Summary: Explains the virtue of prudence, or thinking carefully before acting,
and describes ways to show prudence at home, at school, and in the community.
    Includes bibliographical references (p. 24) and index.
    ISBN 0-7368-0510-9
    1. Prudence—Juvenile literature. 2. Children—Conduct of life—Juvenile
literature. [1. Prudence.] I. Title. II. Series.
BJ1533.P9 R33 2000
179'.9—dc21   99-048334

Editorial Credits

Sarah Schuette, editor; Steve Christensen, cover designer; Kimberly Danger,
    photo researcher

Photo Credits

David F. Clobes, 4, 16
FPG International LLC, 18
International Stock/Earl Kogler, cover; Scott Barrow, 20
Marilyn Mosely LaMantia, 12, 14
Matt Swinden, 8
Photo Network, 10
Uniphoto, 6

1 2 3 4 5 6 05 04 03 02 01 00

Table of Contents

Prudence

Prudence means thinking carefully before acting. Prudent people consider all choices before making decisions. For example, you may want to drink soda. But you know juice is better for you. Thinking carefully helps prudent people make good decisions.

decision

a choice; making a decision means making up your mind.

Being Prudent

Be prudent by thinking before you act. You may want to bake a cake. But the oven is very hot. Show prudence by asking an adult to help you with the oven. You are prudent when you avoid danger.

avoid

to stay away from something

Being Prudent at Home

Prudent people use problem-solving skills. Think about a family problem that you need to solve. Talk to your family. Make a list of possible solutions to the problem. Think of what will happen with each solution. Pick the solution that will work the best.

solution

the answer to a problem

Prudence with Your Friends

You are prudent with your friends when you show caution. Try hard to avoid danger. Wear a helmet when you ride a skateboard or a bicycle. Wear safety equipment when you play sports. Showing prudence with your friends will keep you safe.

caution
carefulness or watchfulness

Prudence and Your Resources

Prudent people use their resources well. You are prudent when you take care of your toys. Playing roughly with toys can break them. You are prudent when you think carefully before spending money. Save money for something you really want. Buy only what you need.

resource
something valuable or useful

Prudence at School

Planning ahead can help you do better in school. Schoolwork can be hard. Be prudent by planning your schoolwork ahead of time. Gather things you need for projects early instead of at the last minute. Study early for tests.

Prudence in Your Community

You need to make good decisions in your community. Be careful around strangers. Do not walk alone at night. Walk across the street instead of biking. Use the crosswalks. You are prudent when you are careful in your community.

"A penny saved is a penny earned."
—Benjamin Franklin

Prudent Benjamin Franklin

Benjamin Franklin was an inventor and a leader of the United States. Benjamin wrote books full of prudent advice. He saved money wisely. His inventions helped make life easier for people. Benjamin tried hard to improve his character and to live prudently.

advice

a suggestion about
what someone should do

Prudence and You

Taking time to think and to make the right choices may be hard. Prudent people plan ahead. They dress warmly in cold weather. You are prudent when you make good choices. Showing prudence will help you be happy, safe, and successful.

Hands On: Making a Budget

Spending money carefully and saving money is an important part of being prudent. A budget is a plan for saving and spending money.

A piece of paper
A pencil
Two jars or other containers

1. Draw three columns on the piece of paper. Label the columns "money,""spending," and "savings."
2. Write the amount you expect to receive each month in the money column.
3. In the spending column, make a list of things you plan to buy and their costs. Add these costs together. These costs are your expenses.
4. Subtract this amount from the money column. This is the total money you have left after expenses.
5. You can save the amount of money you have left. Write this amount in the savings column. Subtract this amount from the money column. Your amount in the money column should now be zero.
6. Label one jar spending. Label one jar savings. Put the money for the amounts you have written down into each jar.

Words to Know

advice (ad-VICE)—a suggestion about what someone should do

avoid (uh-VOID)—to stay away from something

caution (KAW-shun)—carefulness or watchfulness

decision (di-SIZH-uhn)—a choice; making a decision means making up your mind.

equipment (i-KWIP-muhnt)—the tools used in a sport

resource (ri-SORSS)—something valuable or useful; your resources may include clothes, toys, and money.

solution (suh-LOO-shuhn)—the answer to a problem

Read More

Otfinoski, Steven. *The Kid's Guide to Money: Earning It, Saving It, Spending It, Growing It, Sharing It.* New York: Scholastic, 1996.

Usel, T. M. *Benjamin Franklin.* A Photo-Illustrated Biography. Mankato, Minn.: Bridgestone Books, 1996.

Internet Sites

Decision-Making Skills for Young People
http://www.crossnet.org/tips/april/aprtip99.html
KidsBank.com
http://www.kidsbank.com
NHTSA's Safety City
http://www.nhtsa.dot.gov/kids/
The World of Benjamin Franklin
http://sln.fi.edu/franklin/rotten.html

Index

Growing Readers
New Hanover County
Public Library
201 Chestnut Street
Wilmington, NC 28401